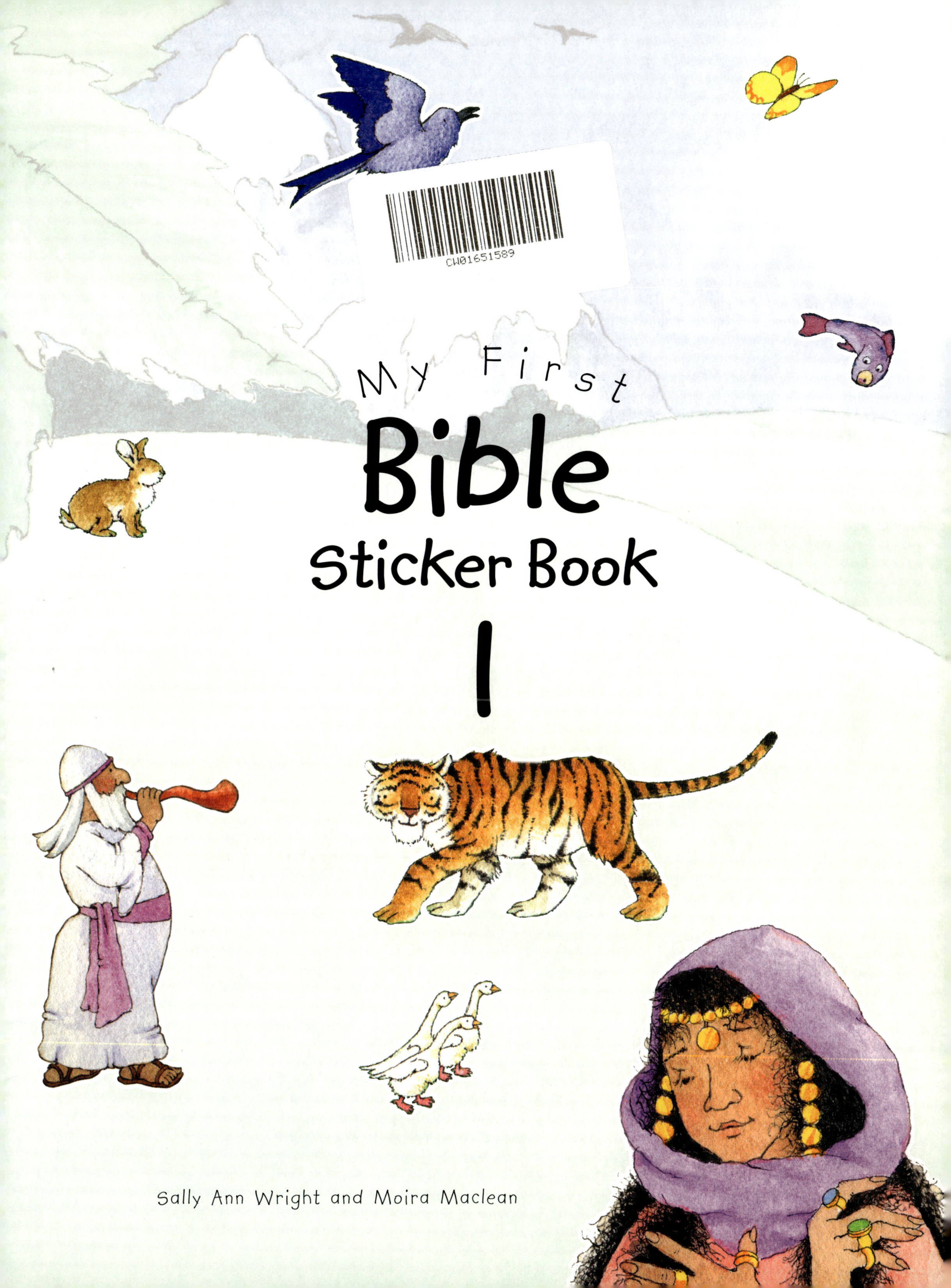

My First

Bible Sticker Book 1

Sally Ann Wright and Moira Maclean

A beautiful world

In the beginning, God made light to shine in the darkness.

God formed the land with tall mountains and deep blue seas. God made sweet-smelling flowers and leafy trees.

God gave his world a red hot sun and a silvery moon.

He made stars and planets to twinkle in the night sky.

God filled the seas with slippery fish and the air with beautiful birds. God made animals that moved on the land and swung through the trees. Then God made people to be his friends.

God was pleased with everything he had made. It was very good.

The walls of Jericho

Many years passed. Not everyone listened to God and the world became a place where people were greedy and often hurt each other.

God promised to give his people a special land that they could call their own.

God asked Joshua to take his people into Canaan.

But first they had to get past the strong, high walls of Jericho where the people were fierce and unfriendly.

God told Joshua what to do and he followed God's instructions. After seven days, the priests blew on their trumpets... and all the people shouted... and the walls of the city tumbled to the ground!

Daniel and the lions

Daniel worked hard for the king of Babylon. He also loved God and prayed to him every day.

Other men were jealous of Daniel. The men told the king to make a law so that praying to God must stop.

'Anyone who prays to God must be thrown to the lions!' they said.

Daniel prayed just as he had always done. So he was taken to the lions' den.

The king liked Daniel. In the morning, he went to see if Daniel was still alive. Could his God have saved him?

'God sent an angel to close the lions' mouths!' Daniel said. 'The one true God has saved me.'

Esther, the beautiful queen

King Xerxes chose Esther to be his queen because she was very beautiful, but he did not know that she loved God.

There was a man called Haman at the palace who thought himself very important. Haman hated God's people. He planned to kill

2
4
8
6
3
8
12
2
7
10
15
10
14
12
14
8
7
4
2

15
11
5
12
9
7
6
10
15
14
5
9
11
13
11
3
7

them all with the King's permission.

Esther's cousin told her about the plan, and Esther told King Xerxes that she was one of God's people – and that Haman was going to kill them all.

The King was very angry and gave orders for Haman to be killed instead.

Esther the beautiful queen had saved God's people.

The storm on the lake

Jesus taught people that God loved them. He healed people who needed help. He showed them how to care about other people.

One day, Jesus sailed across Lake Galilee with his friends. He was very tired and soon fell asleep.

Suddenly a storm blew up, battering the little boat and filling it with water.

'Help us, Jesus!' his friends shouted.

But Jesus was still asleep.

'Help us, or we'll drown!' they shouted again.

Jesus woke up and spoke to the wind and the raging storm. Soon all was quiet again. Jesus' friends were amazed. Jesus had power over the wind and the waves.

Jesus heals a blind man

Bartimaeus could not see. He sat by the side of the road every day, hoping someone would give him money so he could eat.

One day he heard the noise of a big crowd. Jesus was coming! Bartimaeus had heard about how Jesus helped people.

'Jesus! Help me!' Bartimaeus called out.

The people in the crowd frowned at him. But Jesus stopped. Jesus listened.

'How can I help you?' Jesus asked.

'I want to see!' Bartimaeus said.

'Go,' Jesus said. 'You can see!'

Bartimaeus jumped up! He could see! He was so happy, he followed Jesus.

Jesus, the King

Jesus knew that soon he would be arrested by men who were jealous of him. But he still had work to do for God. There were still things to teach his friends.

First, he must go to Jerusalem.

Jesus sent two of his friends into a village where he knew a donkey and her colt were waiting for him.

His friends spread their cloaks on them so Jesus could ride into Jerusalem on the donkey.

Crowds of people were waiting for him. They waved palm branches and cheered. Others spread cloaks as well as palms on the ground in front of him.

'Here comes Jesus! Hooray for Jesus the king!'

Published in the UK by The Bible Reading Fellowship
First Floor, Elsfield Hall, 15-17 Elsfield Way, Oxford OX2 8FG
ISBN 1 84101 444 3

First edition 2005

Editorial Director Annette Reynolds · Art Director Gerald Rogers.
Pre-production Krystyna Hewitt · Production John Laister

British Library Cataloguing in Publication Data.
A catalogue record for this book is available from the British Library.

Printed and bound in China